C000292565

BE MORE
HARRY

CONTENTS

INTRODUCTION

There was once a boy, standing alone on a stage, about to be catapulted to pop stardom. All these years later, despite having an incredible career and regularly being called "the most handsome man in the world," Harry has a reputation for being the politest person in music (and Hollywood). And he's done it all without losing any of his unique sparkle.

The natural charm that radiates from Harry like rays of sunshine got him his shot at success, and hard work and good choices have turned him into the superstar he is. So what's his trick for remaining chill while having a face (and hair and tattoos) recognized all over the world? The secret lies in staying true to himself by making music that he loves and rejecting outdated codes that dictate what a man should dress and act like.

Let's step into his golden boots and glitter suits, lean into what makes you, you, and look at 25 ways to be more Harry.

DISCLAIMER
This book has not been written or endorsed by Harry Styles. It was created for Harries, by Harries. It is a love letter to Harry and all those who feel a connection to him.

CHAPTER 1

BE

BOLD

You need to only look at his stage costumes to understand that Harry doesn't do things by halves. He loves to draw attention, and that's a big part of what makes him a great performer. We so often minimize ourselves to avoid attracting negative attention—or even any attention at all. But try living at your own maximum brightness setting. After all, why apologize for living a life that you love?

"I do think some people make their own luck, but I also think so much of it's about luck and timing."

TAKE THE CHANCE

Certain stars need to align for special things to happen.
Yes, you need talent (or at least passion) to be successful.
But that's not everything. Sometimes you also need to be in
the right place at the right time. Back in 2010, Harry's mom
entered him into a singing competition, presumably not even
imagining quite what a life-changing decision that would be for
their family. Harry had the drive, sparkle, and supportive mom,
but he still needed a bit of luck on his side. The opportunity for
a 16-year-old to sing in front of thousands of people at his first
audition is rare enough. The likelihood of capturing the interest
of a powerful and notoriously grumpy music mogul is rarer still.
Opportunities might not always appear in the way you expect...
Harry didn't make it through *The X Factor* auditions as a solo
artist, but it turned out what the world was waiting for was
a new boy band. Keep an eye out for the opportunities all
around you. Who knows where they might lead?

"I wanted to make some decisions for myself."

FOLLOW YOUR OWN PATH

Kids: they grow up, fly the nest, join the most successful boy band of their generation, and then strike out on their own. For Harry, leaving his family behind to embark on a pop career was one thing, but life in a band means you're still making choices together—kind of like a family. Harry says about being in One Direction, "I don't feel like I was held back at all. It was so much fun." But the time came when—sorry if you're not ready to hear this—the band was over, and he had to figure out his own path. You really become an adult when you start making your own decisions. As hard as that transition can be, it's a wonderful moment. You and those you've shared that journey with so far, whether it's bandmates or siblings, get to grow into the people you were born to be.

"If you're not enjoying something
and need to do something else,
you absolutely should do that."

PUT YOUR HAPPINESS FIRST

The thing about humans is that we'll spend ages being slightly unhappy before we take any action. Harry loved being in 1D, but not everyone finds their place in the world so early in life. From the earliest days of *The X Factor*, Zayn found the immense pressures of pop stardom tough to handle. At first, Harry may have been disappointed when Zayn left the band unexpectedly, but he seems to have understood that his longtime friend and colleague just wasn't enjoying it anymore. And when you're not enjoying something, even if everyone else thinks you've got the greatest job in the world, you're allowed to change your life in order to become happier. If you're struggling to accept someone else's decision to pursue their happiness, try and put yourself in their shoes—one size does not fit all.

"There's so many jobs that didn't used to be jobs... If there's something that you really love, you have to just kind of do that... I think you can try and find some way that you can make it a career."

THINK OUTSIDE THE BOX

Not everyone can have a cool job like pop star, spy, or
rhythmic gymnast. And if listening to "Falling" ten times
in a row while weeping was measured against a set of
workplace targets instead of being "for fun," it might ruin it.
But there might actually be a way to turn your interests into
a job without spoiling it. Many people who have run fan accounts
have taken that experience and turned it into a career in digital
media. Harry himself used to sing in the car just to entertain his
family, and now he tours the world sharing his love of music and
sparkly peak-lapel suits. So should you try to turn your passion
into your career? Keep doing the things you love, and keep
an open mind about where it might take you. Ten years ago,
social media barely existed. We can't guess what skills
will be needed in another ten years. That perfect job
could actually be looking for you.

"I realized relatively early on that the whole 'trying to please everyone' thing just doesn't work."

SUIT YOURSELF

How does someone write a number one single? These days it's often engineered to be an exact length, to work on TikTok, and, most of all, to not be too different from what's already on the radio. You can't accuse Harry of courting the mass market. His debut single "Sign of the Times" is nearly six minutes long. Compare that to most commercial pop songs, which are typically around the three-minute mark. Although this was a bold choice, Harry was still finding his feet as an artist and as a person. His first album had a rock sound, and the lyrics contained some rock star posturing about getting girls that didn't fit with the respectful king we know Harry to be. He says now, "I was playing it safe, because I just didn't want to get it wrong." Things get better when you figure out who you are and what you like and honor that—a true fan (or friend) won't ask you to make yourself smaller to please the crowd.

CHAPTER 2

LIGHT UP

YOUR WORLD

It might seem like celebrities have it all figured out, but they feel the heat, too. Often, the more people expect from you, the greater the pressure. Everyone can benefit from talking through their feelings, no matter whether you think the problem is serious enough or whether you "deserve" help. Learn to make time for yourself, and take care of your mental health with a few thoughtful tips from Harry.

"I felt so much weight in terms of not getting things wrong... Now, I feel like the fans have given me an environment to be myself and grow up and create this safe space to learn and make mistakes."

GO EASY ON YOURSELF

It's easy to be hard on ourselves when we make a mistake. One wrong note in the middle of a hundred perfect ones might feel like it ruins the song. It's even worse when you feel like other people are relying on you or you start comparing yourself to other people. Harry's a great singer, but it was never going to be easy for 1D to replace a vocalist like Zayn, whose pipes were crafted by angels. Harry's voice is warm and soulful, so whether he's singing about lost love or fruit, you believe him. He's practiced and improved over time through trial and error. If you're never metaphorically trying to hit that top note in "Diana" and failing, you're not getting out of your comfort zone. Instead of getting hung up on your own missteps, or those of others, try and see them as learning experiences.

"

I'm discovering how much better it makes me feel to be open with friends. Feeling that vulnerability, rather than holding everything in.

"

OPEN UP TO PEOPLE

If, like Harry, you're used to being the life and soul of the party, it can feel scary to admit that you're going through a tough time of sadness, grief, or even anger. That's not what people know you for, and they might get confused if you suddenly start talking about issues like anxiety or loss. Part of becoming more vulnerable is figuring out who is a safe person to talk to about what you're feeling. Don't be discouraged if it doesn't go brilliantly the first time. It can actually be easier to test out vulnerability on someone you don't know that well, where the stakes feel lower. Eventually, you can share vulnerable moments with friends. Being vulnerable is not about venting— it's about creating a safe, trusting space where you and another person are able to talk honestly. In a very real way, it's like writing a song—you're sharing a small, tender part of yourself in an effort to connect with others.

"I had a hard time getting out of my own way enough to go to therapy in the first place."

IT'S OKAY TO ASK FOR HELP

Although it's important to share with your friends and family, some issues are bigger than they can handle. Mental health issues like depression or eating disorders can be really scary for you and the people who love you. If you have access to therapy, a professional can help you look at what's going on, and you don't have to worry about making them feel sad or worried—they can handle it! Like Harry, some people have hang-ups at first about asking for professional help and worry that it makes them weak. Therapy isn't going to solve your problems for you, but it can help you understand them better and develop healthy habits and ways of coping. No one should have to spend years feeling low and dealing with it alone.

"I think meditation has helped with worrying about the future less, and the past less."

LET GO

Harry is a total hippie, as we can tell from his flares, crafty knits, and '70s-infused soft rock on "Canyon Moon." He's up for trying all the latest superfoods and has probably had his star chart done. (He's an Aquarius with a Libra moon, which makes sense—he's unique and loves beautiful things.) Harry's on the record saying that he meditates, especially when he's stressed or can't sleep. He's even narrated a "sleep story" to help you drift off. Meditation is easy to get into, and there's no right way to do it. Give a guided meditation activity a go, or if you find it hard to just sit with your thoughts, you could try taking a walk in nature or going for a swim. When there's no screen or other noise getting between you and your thoughts, you are able to listen to yourself properly.

"This isn't the first time we've been in a hard time, and it's not going to be the last time."

SEE THE BIGGER PICTURE

It feels like the world is spinning faster and faster all the time. You've probably been through some terrible events in your life already—things that changed you, and the world, forever. It can feel like we're living through a uniquely awful moment in history. But although there are big issues to worry about, from climate change (which Harry calls "our biggest issue right now") to racism and transphobia, humanity has been through really bad times before. We made it through because we're smart and adaptable. But that doesn't mean we can rely on human ingenuity alone to avoid catastrophe. Before you start to get overwhelmed, it is not your job to save the world single-handed. But you have moral choices to make and a voice to use, so use it.

CHAPTER 3

KEEP YOUR

FRIENDS CLOSE

Harry has often spoken about the importance of friendship in his life. We're often told that romantic love will complete us, but we need many people to fulfill us, not just one. Channel Harry, and be the friend you'd love to have by making time for the people you like having around. There's a saying that new friends are silver, but old friends are gold. Hang on to your friends from school (or, you know, your boy band), but stay open to new connections that reflect the person you've become.

"... when the band stopped, I realized that the thing I'd been missing, because it was all so fast paced, was human connection."

STAY IN TOUCH

It must be incredible to look out at a stadium full of people screaming your name, to hop on a plane to every beautiful country you've ever wanted to visit, and to hear your songs on the radio. But musicians work *hard*. Being in a boy band is particularly tough, because label bosses know there's a time limit on their appeal, so they work almost nonstop. One Direction's five albums were recorded in bland hotel rooms or in the back of a van—a far cry from the beautiful studios that Harry records in now. These days, he's figured out that you have to enjoy the ride and stay connected, so he records in places like Jamaica and Japan, writing songs with other musicians, watching rom-coms, and just generally having a good time. Like all of us, stars get homesick and lonely when they're far away from their family and friends, but life is full of chances to make connections if you're open to them.

"It's good to have people who can tell you you're an idiot and tell you when you're wrong. I think that's as important as having people geeing you up sometimes."

TAKE THE ROUGH WITH THE SMOOTH

Learning to take feedback is really hard, but it's also really useful. If you like to make things, whether it's crafts or videos, you're going to get feedback from other people. When you're invested in something—even if it's a work task—it can make you feel really stressed and annoyed when people don't immediately like it. Making an album is a process of being told things aren't quite good enough over and over until it finally sounds right. "Watermelon Sugar" took more than a year to get right! Someone's unenviable job was to tell Harry Styles that his song wasn't good enough yet. But if he'd stopped trying to make it better after one day, it wouldn't have ended up as the number one, Grammy-winning treat it is now. Smart people will take the time to give you constructive criticism, not because they think you've made something bad, but because they believe you can do even better. Even smarter people will listen and use the feedback to grow.

"[Lizzo is] so positive, and I try and be pretty positive most of the time, and I think there's some joy in that."

SEE THE GOOD IN OTHERS

Lizzo is a classically-trained musician with a bubbly personality. The more soft-spoken Harry learned his craft at the university of life. But they are united by a cheeky sense of humor and an ability to look on the bright side. Harry and Lizzo have both helped to shatter the taboo around mental health by speaking frankly about the challenges they face. What makes "Hizzo" a fan favorite, though, is their mutual appreciation of each other's talent. Lizzo has been 100% transparent about her love for H: "My favorite British import would be Harry Styles." Meanwhile, Harry has covered her song "Juice" and says Lizzo is "exactly what you want an artist to be." Imagine if all friendships were this obviously based on respect and admiration. People who see the best in you bring out the best in you. So whether you're the Lizzo (the funny one) or the Harry (the one who laughs at the jokes) in the friendship, find people whose energy makes yours sing.

"... music is where I let that cross over. It's the only place, strangely, where it feels right to let that cross over."

KEEP YOUR BOUNDARIES CLEAR

Where do you draw the line between "personal" and "private?" While he probably does have a group chat where he vents about dating, Harry prefers to publicly spill about his relationships only through his music. His songs often contain clues about his love life, some more subtle than others. There has been speculation that the gentle ballad "Two Ghosts" and the 1D anthem "Perfect" are payback for being dragged into another popstar's narrative. They're not all mysterious, though: "Carolina" is about a girl from... Carolina. Despite having been described in the press as a "ladies' man" ever since he was just 16, Harry dodges questions about his exes and tries to speak about them respectfully in public. As for being the inspiration for some of the greatest pop songs ever written, he says humbly, "To have been part of a moment that means something to someone enough for them to write a song about it is a huge compliment."

"The one subject that hits the hardest is
love, whether it's platonic, romantic,
loving it, gaining it, losing it..."

LIVE OUT LOUD

Harry Styles's favorite movie is *The Notebook*—the story of an epic love found, then lost, and finally found again. Featuring one of cinema's greatest on-screen kisses, watching this too many times might set the bar for relationships impossibly high.

In reality, a love story often doesn't work out like it does in the movies, and your perfect person almost certainly doesn't look like Ryan Gosling or Rachel McAdams. But however it happens, one of our jobs in life is to let love happen to us. It doesn't have to last forever to be important. As Harry says, when a relationship ends, whether it's after a week or a year, "You're celebrating the fact it was powerful and made you feel something." And it doesn't need to be romantic to make a big impact on you. Close friendships can be just as important as any romantic relationship, and losing them can feel just as hard. Instead of trying to avoid the emotional blows, let them land, because that's how you get to feel something.

CHAPTER 4

TREAT EVERYONE

EQUALLY

A huge part of what makes Harry so special is that he doesn't just take all the love people give him—he gives it right back to his fans. He knows that showing solidarity with other people and being welcoming of everyone doesn't take anything away from us—in fact, it gives us strength. And when he's criticized himself, he's able to take it on the chin and respond with a cheeky clapback that just makes us adore him even more.

"If you are black, if you are white, if you are gay, if you are straight, if you are transgender —whoever you are, whoever you want to be, I support you."

PRACTICE ACCEPTANCE

The world is full of prejudice. People of color, the LGBTQ+
community, and other marginalized groups face many hurdles.
Their struggles have been shaped by history and risk being
carried into the future by the choices we make today. When
he stated his love and acceptance of marginalized people,
Harry sent a powerful message to his fans and to the world.
But he didn't stop at general statements of inclusivity. Harry
attended a Black Lives Matter march in 2020, donated money
to bail funds, and said "being not racist is not enough, we
must be anti-racist." His strategy is to treat people with
kindness and respect at the personal level but not to forget
about the bigger systems that need to change.

The White Album

"We're so past that dumb outdated narrative of 'Oh, these people are girls, so they don't know what they're talking about.' They're the ones who know what they're talking about."

44

YOUR INTERESTS ARE GOOD ENOUGH

Harry owes his success to the tastes and enthusiasms of girls. From the very first fans to turn up and scream during *The X Factor* auditions, to those who started to take notice during the fun and flamboyant *Fine Line* era, Harry's career has been shaped by what girls like. There are plenty of handsome pop stars, but Harry is more than just good-looking—there's something about him that makes us feel at home. So many things that girls love get dismissed as silly or "basic," but, in reality, girls and women drive the music industry and set careers in motion through sheer fan power. Without our incredible talent-spotting skills, the world would never have gotten to know The Beatles or Taylor Swift. Harry is right that this dismissive attitude is outdated, but it sadly continues. Don't let anyone tell you your interests—whether they're stereotypically "girly" or otherwise—are silly. Whatever you get joy from is valid.

"I'm just trying to make people feel included and seen."

MAKE SPACE FOR OTHERS

Being an ally to others involves more listening than talking.
Everyone who meets Harry, whether it's at a starry reception
or in the street, says that he is very courteous and kind. It's
incredible that he can maintain this energy after a decade of
being asked for autographs every time he leaves the house!
If he can do it, so can we. If you're talking to someone who
has less power in society—or even just in your classroom or
workplace—it pays to listen to what they're going through, and
ask if there's anything you can do. It's not about you right now.
You don't always need to understand what someone is feeling
or agree with how they're expressing it to be supportive.
Really listening is an act of kindness in itself.

"What women wear. What men wear. For me
it's not a question of that... I think the moment
you feel more comfortable with yourself,
it all becomes a lot easier."

JUST WEAR WHATEVER YOU WANT, DUDE

When you think about it, it's actually very weird that there are rigid codes for what men and women are supposed to wear. You need the same protection from the elements and ability to carry stuff around in your pockets regardless of your gender. But as women's fashion is currently more beautiful and colorful than men's, it makes total sense that someone as stylish as Harry would want in on the action. Why are women "allowed" to wear jeans and a T-shirt, but men are not supposed to wear dresses? It's because "women's" clothes and shoes are actually viewed as frivolous and inferior, even when they're sold to us as liberating. Let's break all the "rules." If you want to wear a gorgeous, tiered gown, then do it. But if you want to wear stompy boots and a tuxedo, go ahead. It doesn't make you any less, no matter how you identify. In fact, based on Harry's *Vogue* cover, it could be your most triumphant look ever.

"Don't let anyone tell you who you're supposed to be. Don't let anyone tell you what you're supposed to do with your body. Let's have each other's backs, and look out for each other. And if we do it, I think we'll be alright."

SHOW SOLIDARITY

Harry believes you should have total control over your body. That means no one else should ever be able to touch you in a way you don't consent to. It also means you have the right to equal health care, including reproductive rights. There's no cheerful way to talk about how the rights of women, non-binary, and trans people are being threatened, but it's awesome to have someone like Harry speaking up about it. It's not necessarily easy for him to do so—have you ever noticed how things get tense when serious issues about women's lives come up in conversation? Or how brutal the arguments are around simple things like trans people asking for their correct pronoun to be used? Our bodies should not be a battleground. But Harry has your back. So when someone does try to overstep one of your boundaries, remember that you are the only person who gets to choose what's right for you.

CHAPTER 5

DANCE LIKE

NOBODY'S WATCHING

You've heard of the art of painting, but did you know there's an art of living? From the beautiful objects you surround yourself with—a Harry Styles prayer candle really sets the tone—to the experiences you curate, it's all about crafting a joyful life. One of the most Harry things ever are the "boops" at the end of "Sunflower Vol. 06." Those few silly noises represent how he's liberated himself to do whatever he wants. It really doesn't matter where you find your joy, but you owe it to yourself to find your unique, personal boops.

"If you're happy doing what you're doing, then nobody can tell you you're not successful."

REDEFINE WHAT SUCCESS MEANS TO YOU

We all grow up learning that life is like an open road. As you drive along, you'll pass all of life's milestones, from graduating high school to marriage. What nobody tells you is that the road map is made-up. Just totally invented. All those markers of "life success" might mean a lot to someone else, but do they actually mean something to you? When Harry talks about the kind of success he is supposed to want, he means playing huge stadiums or having number one records. But if playing intimate venues and making music that he loves make him happier, that's a truer form of success to him. Your personal success road map might include adopting a pair of rabbits, climbing the tallest mountain in your country, or getting a tattoo of Harry dressed as Dorothy from *The Wizard of Oz*. These are all valid goals. Try making some lists of cool stuff you dream of doing. No time limits, no pressure—just you living your wildest, sparkliest, most YOU life.

"Life's too short.
It should just be fun."

DON'T BE AFRAID TO BE SILLY

After singing and looking really good in photos, Harry's third biggest talent is having fun. He seems to always be jumping into a pool or a lake or the sea. His jokes are legendarily weak, but he keeps telling them. Whether it's playing soccer with his friends or feeling the wind in his curls on the back of a speedboat, Harry seeks out the fun in life. Even his clothing choices speak to this part of his personality—from sweaters with cartoon sheep on them to 1970s fishing apparel, he wears pieces with a sense of humor. It's easy for us all to get hung up on the humdrum details of life—like worrying about exams or what your boss thinks about you—and forget to take breaks. Don't let busy, stressful days become a long and boring life. Make space for fun, whatever that means to you. Dance in front of the mirror to "What Makes You Beautiful" every now and then. Or make your friends watch you do the dance. Whatever works.

66

... **people want to see me experiment and have fun. Nobody wants to see you fake it.**

99

KEEP IT REAL

Keeping the weirder, quirkier parts of yourself hidden away inside is a good survival technique... for a while. When you look back at photos of yourself in the past, you can probably see the ways you've tried to fit in. Maybe you straightened your hair or your mannerisms. Don't blame yourself for doing what made you feel safe in the past. Harry's whole "bad boy in skinny jeans and band T-shirt" era was cool at the time—it just wasn't the whole story. You can find out who you really are step-by-step. Try a new hobby that brings you into contact with new kinds of people. Imagine your dream outfit—the one you wouldn't dare wear in real life—and work toward being confident enough to pull it off. Listen to music outside of your normal playlists, and read books you don't expect to like. Life is an experiment, and every little risk helps you grow.

"Ultimately, I think if you wear something and you're confident with it then it's gonna look better than... stuff wearing you."

MAKE IT YOUR OWN

Clothes can be thoughtfully designed and beautifully made, but they aren't stylish when they're just hanging on a rack. It takes a person to bring them to life. If you've never sat down and defined your style, it's a really fun exercise. Start by picking a color palette you love or seeing which aesthetic you are drawn to. Understanding your own taste—instead of being overly influenced by trends—helps you pick outfits intentionally, which helps you buy fewer things and value them more, which helps the environment. Harry's influence on our style tends to be less about rushing out to buy exact copies and more about channeling his joyful approach. Thousands of people knitted brightly colored patchwork cardigans like Harry's after craftswoman Liv Huffman showed how to make one on TikTok. These homemade efforts weren't perfect replicas. They were more like cover versions. Harry's cardigan is now on display in the Victoria & Albert Museum in London—right next to Liv's.

"I always said, at the very beginning,
all I wanted was to be the granddad
with the best stories."

YOU ONLY LIVE ONCE

Harry's experienced a lot of life for someone so young. He's traveled all over the world and performed in front of massive crowds. He's faced camera flashes and public opinion, and he's turned his private experiences into songs. Even if he retired tomorrow (which he won't—he's still got to win an Academy Award), he would have enough stories to tell for the rest of his life. Even if you aren't living life as intensely as Harry, time can still flash past you in the blink of an eye. Take a minute, ideally once a day, to slow down and be in the moment. Write down three things you're grateful for and at least one thing you like about your life right now. You have a lot to be proud of! Life is made up of experiences, which turn into memories, which become your story. Obviously, it would be great to be more Harry—more confident, brave, sparkly, and joyful—but if we've learned anything from him, it's that the most important thing of all is to be more you.

Project Editor Beth Davies
Editor Vicky Armstrong
Designer Isabelle Merry
Senior Production Editor Jennifer Murray
Senior Production Controller Louise Minihane
Managing Editor Pete Jorgensen
Managing Art Editor Jo Connor
Publishing Director Mark Searle

Written by Satu Hämeenaho-Fox
Cover and interior illustrations Nastka Drabot
Additional artwork Isabelle Merry

DK would like to thank
Jennette ElNaggar for proofreading.

Quotations: **p.6** *The Howard Stern Show* (video interview), 2020; **p.8** *Apple Music* (video interview), 2019; **p. 9** *Rolling Stone* (interview), 2019; **p.10** *Rolling Stone* (interview), 2017; **p.12** *The Zoe Ball Breakfast Show* (radio interview), 2020; **p.14** *The Howard Stern Show* (video interview), 2020; **p.15** *Apple Music* (video interview), 2019; **p.18** *Rolling Stone* (interview), 2019; **p.20** *Apple Music* (video interview), 2019; **p.22** *The Howard Stern Show* (video interview), 2020; **p.24** *Rolling Stone* (interview), 2019; **p.26** *Rolling Stone* (interview), 2017; **p. 27** *Total Access* (video interview), 2019; **p.30** *The Guardian* (interview), 2019; **p.32** *Another Man* (interview), 2018; **p.34** *Syke On Air* (video interview), 2020; **p.35** *Metro* (article), 2020; *Rolling Stone* (article), 2019; **p.36** *Rolling Stone* (interview), 2019; **p.37** *Harry Styles: Behind the Album* (documentary), 2017; **p.38** *Rolling Stone* (interview), 2017; **p.39** *Rolling Stone* (interview), 2017; **p.42** *Rolling Stone* (interview), 2019; **p.43** *Elle.com* (article), 2020; **p.44** *Rolling Stone* (interview), 2019; **p.46** *Rolling Stone* (interview), 2019; **p.48** *The Guardian* (interview), 2019; **p.50** *Love on Tour* tour (speech), 2021; **p.54** *Apple Music* (video interview), 2020; **p.56** *Syke On Air* (video interview), 2020; **p.58** *Rolling Stone* (interview), 2019; **p.60** *Syke On Air* (video interview), 2020; **p.62** *Rolling Stone* (interview), 2017

First published in Great Britain in 2022 by
Dorling Kindersley Limited
DK, One Embassy Gardens, 8 Viaduct Gardens,
London SW11 7BW

The authorised representative in the EEA is
Dorling Kindersley Verlag GmbH. Arnulfstr. 124,
80636 Munich, Germany

10 9 8 7 6 5
005–332167–May/2022

A CIP catalogue record for this book is
available from the British Library.
ISBN 978-0-2415-7331-0

Printed and bound in China

For the curious
www.dk.com

This book was made with
Forest Stewardship Council™
certified paper – one small
step in DK's commitment
to a sustainable future.